CURRICULUM AND EVALUATION

S T A N D A R D S

FOR SCHOOL MATHEMATICS

ADDENDA SERIES, GRADES K–6

S I X T H - G R A D E B O O K

Grace Burton   Jeane Joyner

Douglas Clements   Miriam A. Leiva

Terrence Coburn   Mary M. Lindquist

John Del Grande   Lorna Morrow

John Firkins

Miriam A. Leiva, Series Editor

NATIONAL COUNCIL OF
TEACHERS OF MATHEMATICS

Copyright © 1992 by
THE NATIONAL COUNCIL OF TEACHERS OF MATHEMATICS, INC.
1906 Association Drive, Reston, Virginia 22091-1593

Second printing 1993

Library of Congress Cataloging-in-Publication Data:

Sixth-grade book / Grace Burton . . . [et al.].
        p.   cm. — (Curriculum and evaluation standards for school
mathematics addenda series. Grades k–6)
    Includes bibliographical references.
    ISBN 0-87353-316-X
    1. Mathematics—Study and teaching (Elementary) I. Burton, Grace
M. II. National Council of Teachers of Mathematics. III. Series.
QA135.5.S543   1992
372.7—dc20   92-16924
                                                                  CIP

Photographs are by Patricia Fisher; artwork is by Lynn Gohman and Don Christian.

Printed in the United States of America

FOREWORD

The *Curriculum and Evaluation Standards for School Mathematics* (NCTM 1989a) describes a framework for revising and strengthening school mathematics. This visionary document provides a set of guidelines for K–12 mathematics curricula and for evaluating both the mathematics curriculum and students' progress. It not only addresses what mathematics students should learn but also how they should learn it.

As the document was being developed, it became apparent that supporting publications would be needed to interpret and illustrate how the vision could be translated realistically into classroom practices. A Task Force on the Addenda to the Curriculum and Evaluation Standards for School Mathematics, chaired by Thomas Rowan and composed of Joan Duea, Christian Hirsch, Marie Jernigan, and Richard Lodholz, was appointed by Shirley Frye, then NCTM president. The Task Force's recommendations on the scope and nature of the supporting publications were submitted to the Educational Materials Committee, which subsequently framed the Addenda Project.

Central to the Addenda Project was the formation of three writing teams—consisting of classroom teachers, mathematics supervisors, and university mathematics educators—to prepare a series of publications, the Addenda Series, targeted at mathematics instruction in grades K–6, 5–8, and 9–12. The purpose of the series is to clarify and illustrate the message of the *Curriculum and Evaluation Standards.* The underlying themes of problem solving, reasoning, communication, and connections are woven throughout the materials, as is the view of assessment as a means of guiding instruction. Activities have been field tested by teachers to ensure that they reflect the realities of today's classrooms.

It is envisioned that the Addenda Series will be a source of ideas by teachers as they begin to implement the recommendations in the NCTM *Curriculum and Evaluation Standards.* Individual volumes in the series are appropriate for in-service programs and for preservice courses in teacher education programs.

A project of this magnitude required the efforts and talents of many people over an extended time. Sincerest appreciation is extended to the authors and the editor and to the following teachers and mathematics supervisors who played key roles in developing, revising, and trying out the materials for the *Sixth-Grade Book:* Marea Channel, Angela C. Gardner, Jan Luquirre, Cynthia S. Parker, and Merrie Schroeder. Finally, this project would not have materialized without the outstanding technical support supplied by Cynthia Rosso and the NCTM publications staff.

Bonnie H. Litwiller
Addenda Project Coordinator

PREFACE

Something exciting is happening in many elementary school classrooms! A vision of an innovative mathematics program is coming alive. There *is* a shift in emphasis in the teaching and learning of mathematics. Teachers are encouraging children to investigate, discuss, question, and verify. They are focusing on explorations and dialogues. They are using various strategies to assess students' progress. They are making mathematics accessible to all children while exposing them to the value and the beauty of mathematics. Teachers and students are excited, and their enthusiasm is contagious. You can *catch it* when you hear children confidently explaining their solutions to the class, when you see them modeling problems with manipulatives, and when you observe them using a variety of methods and materials to arrive at answers. Some children are working with paper and pencil or with calculators; others are sharpening their estimation and mental math skills. There is noise in these classrooms—the sounds of students actively participating in the class and constructing their own knowledge through experiences that will give them confidence in their own abilities and make them mathematically powerful.

> I remember my own experiences in mathematics in elementary school. The classroom was quiet; all you could hear was the movement of pencils across sheets of paper and an occasional comment from the teacher. I was often bored; work was done in silent isolation, rules were memorized, and many routine problems were worked using rules few of us understood. Mathematics didn't always make sense. It was something that you did in school, mostly with numbers, and that you didn't need outside the classroom.
>
> "Why are we doing this?" my friend whispered.
>
> "Because it's in the book," I replied.
>
> "Do it this way," the teacher would explain while writing another problem on the chalkboard. "When you finish, work the next ten problems in the book."

We must go beyond how we were taught and teach how we wish we had been taught. We must bring to life a vision of what a mathematics classroom should be.

Rationale for Change

These are challenging times for you, the teachers of elementary school mathematics, and for your students. Major reforms in school mathematics are advocated in reports that call for changes in the curriculum, in student and program evaluations, in instruction, and in the classroom environment. These reforms are prompted by the changing needs of our society, which demand that all students become mathematically literate to function effectively in a technological world. A richer mathematics program is also supported by an explosion of new mathematical knowledge—more mathematics has been created in this century than in all our previous history. Research studies on teaching and learning, with emphasis on *how children learn mathematics,* have had a significant impact on current practices and strengthen the case for reform. Advances in technology also dictate changes in content and teaching.

Our students, the citizens of tomorrow, need to learn not only *more* mathematics but also mathematics that is broader in scope. They must have a strong academic foundation to enable them to expand their knowledge, to interpret information, to make reasonable decisions, and to solve increasingly complex problems using various approaches and tools, including calculators and computers. Mathematics instruction must reflect and implement these revised educational goals and increased expectations.

The blueprint for reform is the *Curriculum and Evaluation Standards for School Mathematics* (National Council of Teachers of Mathematics 1989a), which identifies a set of standards for the mathematics curriculum in grades K–12 as well as standards for evaluating the quality of programs and students' performance. The *Curriculum and Evaluation Standards* sets forth a bold vision of what mathematics education in grades K–12 should be and describes how mathematics classrooms can fit the vision.

Mathematics as Sense Making

In the past, mathematics classrooms were dominated by instruction and performance of rote procedures "to get the right answer." The *Curriculum and Evaluation Standards* supports the view of school mathematics as a sense-making experience encompassing a wide range of content, instructional approaches, and evaluation techniques.

Four standards are closely woven into content and instruction: mathematics as problem solving, mathematics as communication, mathematics as reasoning, and mathematical connections. These strands are common themes that support all other standards throughout all grade levels.

A primary goal for the study of mathematics is to give children experiences that promote the ability *to solve problems* and that build mathematics from situations generated within the context of everyday experiences. Students are also expected *to make conjectures and conclusions* and *to discuss their reasoning* in words, both written and spoken; with pictures, graphs, and charts; and with manipulatives. Moreover, students learn *to value mathematics* when they *make connections* between topics in mathematics, between the concrete and the abstract, between concepts and skills, and between mathematics and other areas in the curriculum.

The Changing Roles of Students

Previous efforts to reform school mathematics focused primarily on the curriculum; the *Curriculum and Evaluation Standards* also deals with other factors—in particular, students—that affect and are affected by reforms. The role of students is redirected from passive recipients to active participants, from isolated workers to team members, from listeners to investigators and reporters, and from timid followers to intrepid explorers and risk takers. They are asked to develop, discuss, create, model, validate, and investigate to learn mathematics.

Many people, including students, believe that mathematics is for the privileged few. It is time to dispel that myth. All children, regardless of sex, socioeconomic background, language, race, or ethnic origin, can and must succeed in school mathematics. With proper instruction, encouragement, and high expectations, *all* students can do mathematics.

Your Role in Implementing the Standards

All elementary school teachers are teachers of mathematics. Thus, your role is to build your students' self-confidence and nurture their natural curiosity; to challenge them with rich problems through which they will learn to value mathematics and appreciate the order and beauty of mathematics; to provide them with a strong foundation for further study; and to encourage their mathematical ability and power.

The elementary school years are crucial in a child's cognitive and affective development, and you are the central figure. You structure classroom experiences to implement the curriculum and create a supportive

"When my sixth-grade students had the unit on population density, we studied area, growth rate, projected population, and the use of census data. It gave me a good opportunity to make connections within mathematics and with social studies."

One person per square mile

"My goal is to give all my students the opportunity to succeed in mathematics and to develop the unique talents each of them possesses."

$$1+3+5+7=16$$

environment for learning to take place. In most activities you are the guide, the coach, the facilitator, and the instigator of mathematical explorations.

♦ You give children the gift of self-confidence. Through your careful grouping, astute questions, appropriate tasks, and realistic expectations, each student can experience success.

♦ Long after they forget childhood events, your students will remember you. Your excitement and interest permeate the room and stimulate their appreciation for mathematics.

♦ Through your classroom practices, you promote mathematical thinking, reasoning, and understanding.

♦ You lay the foundation on which further study will take place. You give students multiple strategies and tools to solve problems. The questions you ask and the problems you pose can capture your students' imagination, arouse their curiosity, and encourage their creativity.

♦ You facilitate the building of their knowledge by giving them interesting problems to solve, which leads to the development of concepts and important mathematical ideas.

♦ Rules, algorithms, and formulas emerge from student explorations guided by you, the teacher of mathematics.

Instructional Tools and the Standards

In order to implement the curriculum envisioned in the *Curriculum and Evaluation Standards,* we must carefully select and creatively use instructional tools. The textbook is only one of many important teaching resources. Children's development of concepts is fostered by their extensive use of physical materials to represent and describe mathematical ideas.

Calculators and computers are essential instructional tools at all levels. Through the appropriate use of these tools, students are able to solve realistic problems, investigate patterns, explore procedures, and focus on the steps to solve problems instead of on tedious computations.

Implementing the Evaluation Standards

Evaluation must be an integral part of teaching. A primary component of instruction is an ongoing assessment of what goes on in our classrooms. This information helps us make decisions about what we teach and how we teach it, about students' progress and feelings, and about our mathematics program.

The *Curriculum and Evaluation Standards* advocates many changes in curriculum, in instruction, and in the roles of students and teachers. None of these changes are more important than those related to evaluation. We must learn to use a variety of assessment instruments and not depend on pencil-and-paper tests alone. Tools such as observations, interviews, projects, reports, portfolios, diaries, and tests provide a more complete picture of what children understand and are able to use. Knowing what questions to ask is a skill we must develop.

When we test, we send a message about what we think is important. Because we encourage reasoning and communicating mathematically, we practice these skills. Because manipulatives and calculators are valuable tools for learning, we promote their use in the classroom. Because we want children to experience cooperative problem solving, we provide opportunities for group activities. *Not only must we evaluate what we want children to learn, but also how we want them to learn it.*

You and This Book

This booklet is part of the Curriculum and Evaluation for School Mathematics Addenda Series, Grades K–6. This series was designed to illustrate the standards and to help you translate them into classroom practice through—

♦ sample lessons and discussions that focus on the development of concepts;

♦ activities that connect models and manipulatives with concepts and with mathematical representations;

♦ problems that exemplify the use and integration of technology;

♦ teaching strategies that promote students' reasoning;

♦ approaches to evaluate students' progress;

♦ techniques to improve instruction.

In this booklet, both traditional and new topics are explored in four areas: Patterns, Number Sense and Operations, Making Sense of Data, and Geometry and Spatial Sense.

You will find classic sixth-grade activities that have been infused with an investigative flavor. These experiences include investigating properties of polygons through transformations; reinforcing spatial perception through mental and physical manipulations of figures; posing nonroutine problems that involve estimation, measurement, and numerical operations; using the computer to solve problems and to investigate geometric figures; learning to select appropriate statistical measures; constructing a circle graph with manipulatives and relating the graph to fractions, percents, and angle measure; exploring patterns pictorially and abstractly; and bridging from arithmetic to algebra by investigating patterns, making generalizations, and determining the rule for the nth term in a sequence. Margin notes give you additional information on the activities and on such topics as student self-confidence, evaluation, and grouping. Connections to science, language arts, social studies, and other areas in the curriculum are made throughout. Supporting statements from the *Curriculum and Evaluation Standards* appear as margin notes.

Change is an ongoing process that takes time and courage. It is not easy to go beyond comfort and security to try new things. As you use this book, pick and choose at will, and sample alternative approaches and ideas for instruction and assessment. Savor the freedom of change. All the documents in the world will not effect change in the classrooms; *only you can.*

The Challenge and the Vision

"I wonder why...?"

"What would happen if ...?"   "Tell me about your pattern."

"Can you do it another way?"   "Our group has a different solution."

These inviting words give students the freedom to be creative, the confidence to solve problems, and the power to do mathematics. When you give your students the opportunity to construct their own knowledge, you are opening the doors of mathematics to *all* young learners.

This is the challenge. This is the vision.

Miriam A. Leiva, Editor
K–6 Addenda Series

Math in Our World

$$\frac{a}{b} = 1.618$$

The golden ratio is used by architects to design buildings that are visually appealing.

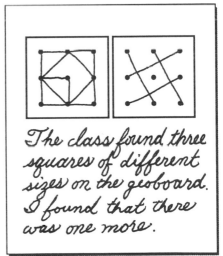

The class found three squares of different sizes on the geoboard. I found that there was one more.

BIBLIOGRAPHY

National Council of Teachers of Mathematics. Curriculum and Evaluation Standards for School Mathematics Addenda Series, Grades K–6, edited by Miriam A. Leiva. Reston, Va.: The Council, 1991–92.

_____. Curriculum and Evaluation Standards for School Mathematics Addenda Series, Grades 5–8, edited by Frances R. Curcio. Reston, Va.: The Council, 1991–92.

_____. Curriculum and Evaluation Standards for School Mathematics Addenda Series, Grades 9–12, edited by Christian R. Hirsch. Reston, Va.: The Council, 1991–92.

_____. Curriculum and Evaluation Standards for School Mathematics. Reston, Va.: The Council, 1989a.

_____. New Directions for Elementary School Mathematics. 1989 Yearbook of the National Council of Teachers of Mathematics. Edited by Paul Trafton. Reston, Va.: The Council, 1989b.

_____. Professional Standards for Teaching Mathematics. Reston, Va.: The Council, 1991.

National Research Council. Everybody Counts: A Report to the Nation on the Future of Mathematics Education. Washington, D.C.: National Academy Press, 1989.

ACKNOWLEDGMENTS

At a time when the mathematics community was looking for directions on implementing the *Curriculum and Evaluation Standards for School Mathematics,* a group of dedicated professionals agreed to serve on the NCTM Elementary Addenda Project.

The task of editing and writing for this series has been challenging and rewarding. Selecting, testing, writing, and editing, as we attempted to translate the message of the *Standards* into classroom practices, proved to be a monumental and ambitious task. It could not have been done without the dedication and hard work of the authors, the teachers who reviewed and field tested the activities, and the editorial team.

My appreciation is extended to the main authors for each topic:

Grace Burton — Number Sense and Operations
Terrence Coburn — Patterns
John Del Grande and Lorna Morrow — Geometry and Spatial Sense
Mary M. Lindquist — Making Sense of Data

Our colleagues in the classrooms, Marea Channel, Angela C. Gardner, Jan Luquirre, Cynthia S. Parker, and Merrie Schroeder, are thanked for giving us the unique perspective of teachers and children.

A special note of gratitude is owed to the individuals who served both as writers and as the editorial panel: Douglas Clements, John Firkins, and Jeane Joyner.

The editor also gratefully acknowledges the strong support of Bonnie Litwiller, Coordinator of the Addenda Project, and the assistance of Cynthia Rosso and the NCTM production staff for their guidance and help through the process of planning and producing this series of books.

Two NCTM presidents, Shirley Frye and Iris Carl, inspired us. A third president, Mary Lindquist, gave countless hours and creative energy to this project. The Addenda Series is a tribute to them.

The greatest reward for all who have contributed to this effort will be the knowledge that the ideas presented here have been implemented in elementary school classrooms, that these ideas have made realities out of visions, and that they have fostered improved mathematics programs for all children.

Miriam A. Leiva

▲ PATTERNS

Generalizing from a pattern is a natural human behavior. Students enjoy the feeling of power that comes when they are able to capture the rhyme or reason to a pattern. This generalization allows them to make predictions. Being acutely aware of the environment and being able to react spontaneously to changing patterns give students a tremendous insight into mathematics and science. Through the study and understanding of patterns, students are able to cope with such changes and to make empowering mathematical connections that place them confidently in control. They get a glimpse of the beauty of mathematics and are curiously interested in what comes next.

In the middle school years, the study of patterns and functions should focus on the interpretation, analysis, representation, and generalization of relationships. These topics should first be explored as informal investigations, using diagrams and pictorial representations whenever needed.

We must make sixth graders see that the study of mathematics is an open invitation to an enormous banquet, a ticket to an exciting and profitable future, and a chance to be prepared for life in the twenty-first century.

Sixth graders should have numerous opportunities to analyze relationships and to attempt written descriptions of relationships by using variables. Many of these students are still concrete thinkers who require some visual stimulation to perceive relationships. Many sixth graders will benefit from the visual and tactile support that manipulatives provide.

BORDER PROBLEMS

Get ready. The purpose of this activity is to have students derive written mathematical expressions. Each pair of students will need square grid paper, markers, scissors, and paper and pencil.

Get going. Prepare a square (e.g., 8 × 8) with its border colored for emphasis. Lead the students to describe the figure and ask:

How many unit squares does it have? [8 × 8, or 64]

How many unit squares are on the border? [28]

Ask for different written mathematical expressions for describing and determining the number of unit squares on the border.

Many students need to have in hand an 8 x 8 square (with the border colored) as they explore ways of writing mathematical expressions for determining the number of unit squares on its border.

*Let the students "own" the
activity:*
*"What is your rule for the
number of squares on the
border?"*
*"Test your rule with some
specific examples."*

Some possible expressions follow:

$$8 + 8 + 6 + 6$$

$$(2 \times 8) + (2 \times 6)$$

$$7 + 7 + 7 + 7$$

$$4 \times 7$$

$$8 + 7 + 7 + 6$$

Have the students cut out a 9×9 square and color the border to illustrate how they thought about the squares on the border.

For example, Terry colored the four corners of his 9×9 square blue and the four segments between the corners yellow. This is what he wrote down:

$$(4 \times 1) + (4 \times 7) = 32$$

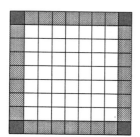

Terry's design

Assign groups of students to explore different figures (6×6, 10×10, and so on) and to find expressions to describe the border. Ask them to find numerical expressions for the number of unit squares in the interior of their squares.

If the number of unit squares in the interior of a square is 81, how many unit squares are there in the square grid? How many are on the boundary?

Can the number of unit squares of a given square grid be 40? Why?

Guide students to find relationships among the number of unit squares in the interior, on the boundary, and in the given square grid.

Keep going. Mathematicians sometimes talk about $n \times n$ squares. What does this mean? Ask,

How many squares are on the border of an $n \times n$ square?

Encourage the students to describe these *n*-squares in several ways. Relate their oral descriptions to a variety of written expressions, such as the following:

$$4 + [4 \times (n - 2)]$$

$$n + n + (n - 2) + (n - 2)$$

$$(n - 1) \times 4$$

$$4 \times n - 4$$

**4 x 7 unit
squares on
the border**

**(8 x 8) – (4 x
7), or 6 x 6,
unit squares
in the interior**

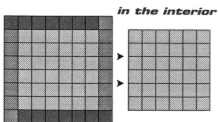

Have the class find expressions to describe and determine the number of unit squares in the interior of an $n \times n$ square once the boundary is known. Help the students with this generalization: In an $n \times n$ square, there are $n \times n$ unit squares with $4 \times (n - 1)$ of these unit squares on the border and $n \times n - 4 \times (n - 1)$ in the interior. The expression $(n - 2) \times (n - 2)$ also describes the number of unit squares in the interior.

THE ODDS ARE SQUARE

Get ready. The purpose of this activity is to have students find numerical patterns for the odd integers. The students are guided to write generalizations for the patterns. Square grid paper, calculators, scissors, pencils, and paper are needed.

Get going. Ask the students to name the consecutive odd integers. [1, 3, 5, 7, . . .] Have them compare the odd integers with the multiples of 2, and help them notice that an odd integer is one more (or less) than an even integer. Place the numbers in a table and investigate the relationships and patterns. Guide the students to describe the *n*th odd integer:

One is first, 3 is second, 5 is third. What is the sixth odd integer? [11]

Have them continue the table and lead them to generalize their results. Show the number 5 as an arrangement in the form of an **L**, with the two legs sharing the corner square. Allow time for pairs of students to cut out a set of consecutive odd numbers—1 through 13—like those at the right.

Encourage the students to describe the odd numbers in terms of these arrangements. For example,

*How many squares are in one leg of the **L** for the number 5?* [3]

What is the third odd number? [5]

What is the relationship between the number of squares in one leg of the arrangement and the odd number it represents? [The *n*th odd number has *n* squares on each leg.]

What connection is there between the fact that there are n squares on each leg and the idea that the nth odd number is "double n minus 1"? [Don't count the corner square twice, i.e., subtract 1.]

Keep going. Ask the students to visualize the sum of the consecutive odd numbers by nesting the **L**s. That is, the first odd number (1) fits in with the second odd number (3) to form a 2 × 2 square that then fits in with the third odd number (5) to form a 3 × 3 square, and so on. Lead them to describe how fitting the **L**s together in this manner is a picture of adding the consecutive odd integers (1 + 3 + 5 + 7 + . . .).

Ask the students to describe the relationship between the sums of consecutive odd integers and the squares that are formed by combining the **L** arrangements. One possible method follows:

$$1 = 1 \times 1$$

$$1 + 3 = 2 \times 2$$

$$1 + 3 + 5 + 7 = 4 \times 4$$

$$1 + 3 + 5 + 7 + 9 = 5 \times 5$$

It may be wise to withhold the use of generalization using the variable (1 + 3 + 5 + 7 + 9 + ... + (2n − 1) = n × n) until the students are ready to suggest it themselves. Revisit this activity throughout the year as you continue to help your students bridge from concrete examples to generalizations and abstract representations.

Another way to explore and reinforce this activity is to have the students use calculators to verify their generalizations.

Sheri entered the first nine odd integers this way:

1 ⊞ 3 ⊞ 5 ⊞ 7 ⊞...⊞ 17 ⊟ (The display showed 81.)

Then she declared, "It's 9 times 9!"

Term Number	1	2	3	4	...	n
Even Number	2	4	6	8	...	2n
Odd Number	1	3	5	7	...	2n−1

"Each odd number is one less than an even number."

1   3   5   7

"Double 3 minus 1 is 5—because you don't want to count the corner square twice."

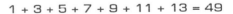

1 + 3 + 5 + 7 + 9 + 11 + 13 = 49

The arrangement of the first seven odd numbers is a 7 x 7 square.

As students work with patterns, you will be able to assess informally their more advanced levels of understanding by asking them to predict beyond what is given or modeled, to generalize, and to suggest situations where similar patterns exist.

Suppose I do not know how many consecutive odd integers were entered? Is there another way to tell how many odd integers are added without counting them? [The last odd integer in the sum above is 17. Seventeen is double 9 minus 1, so there are 9 odd integers in the sum and 9 times 9 is 81.]

If necessary, use a picture to visualize 17 as an **L**.

Have the students choose a square number such as 100, 144, or 225 and subtract consecutive odd integers, beginning with 1, from this square number, keeping count of the number of odd integers subtracted until 0 is obtained.

What do you discover? [If five odd integers are subtracted, the chosen square number was 25.]

Manuel pressed these keys:

121 ⊟ 1 ⊟ 3 ⊟ 5 ⊟ 7 ⊟ ... ⊟ 21 ⊟ (The display showed 0.)

He saw that 21 was the last consecutive odd integer subtracted. Since 21 is the 11th odd integer, or 2(11) − 1, the original square number was 11 × 11, or 121.

CONNECTING TRIANGLE NUMBERS

Get ready. The purpose of this activity is to have students explore triangular numbers. You will need scissors, square grid paper, isometric dot paper, crayons, calculators, and pencils and paper for each pair of students. Students also will need about twenty-five cubes to illustrate some stair steps.

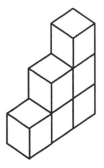

Get going. Build a 3-step with six cubes. Have the students build different step figures. Encourage them to record the number of blocks used for each figure in a table and then use isometric dot paper to draw their figures.

Number of steps	1	2	3	4	5	6
Number of cubes	1	3	6	10	15	21

Now ask the pairs of students to color in "stair steps" on the square grid paper. Allow time for them to illustrate eight different stairs. For a more concrete experience, have the students first use blocks or cubes to build the steps and then color in the stairs on isometric dot paper (p. 32).

How are the pictures of the stairs like the stairs built with cubes?

Ask them to number their figures according to the number of steps each figure has, as illustrated.

Do you notice anything interesting? [The number on the tallest step is the same as the number of blocks.]

Steps	Blocks		
1	1	=	1
2	1 + 2	=	3
3	1 + 2 + 3	=	6
4	1 + 2 + 3 + 4	=	10
.			
.			
.			
n	1 + 2 + ... + *n*	=	

This 3-step stair has 6 blocks.

6 is the third triangular number.

How many blocks are along the bottom row of each figure? [The same number as the number of steps]

How many blocks tall is the tallest step in each figure? [The tallest step is as tall as the same number of blocks on the bottom row.]

How can you determine the total number of blocks in any one figure? [One method: If the figure has 4 steps, add 4 + 3 + 2 + 1.]

What pattern do you see in the numbers in the table? [Students will suggest many different patterns, such as adding the number of steps to the previous number of blocks to get the number of blocks for the current number of steps.]

Keep going. Have the pairs of students form groups of four so that each group has a double set of figures. Ask each pair to cut out their stairs except for the 1-step figure. Have them fit together any two identical figures to form a rectangle.

One group chose two 3-steps. They saw that a 3-step with a 3-step forms a 4 × 3 rectangle. The total number of squares in each 3-step stair is (3 × 4)/2. Ask the students to explore each pair of stairs in the same way, describing the relationship of the number of squares in the rectangle to the number of squares in one set of stair steps.

1 + 2 + 3

has the same sum as

$$\frac{3 \times 4}{2}$$

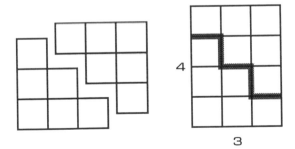

Encourage the students to generalize their patterns with the variable *n* (the number of steps) to obtain an expression for the number of squares in a particular *n*-step figure.

Billy said, "I bet an *n*-step plus an *n*-step makes an $n \times (n + 1)$ rectangle."

Allow the class to explore and discover that the area of the $n \times (n + 1)$ rectangle is the area of two *n*-steps. Therefore, the number of squares in one of the two *n*-steps is $\frac{n \times (n + 1)}{2}$.

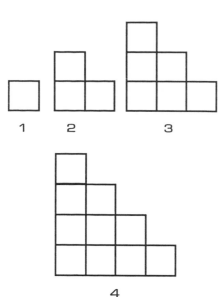

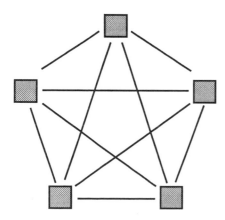

4

1 2 3

What connection is there between the expression for determining the total number of squares in an n-step figure and the numbers in this pattern?

1, 3, 6, 10, 15, 21, 28, 36, …

The numbers in the sequence above are called the triangular numbers. The stair steps resemble isosceles right triangles. The third triangle has six squares, the fourth triangle has ten squares, and so on. Help the students to see that the number of squares in the nth triangle is $n \times (n + 1)$ divided by 2 or that the nth triangular number is $\dfrac{n \times (n + 1)}{2}$.

Use calculators to compute various triangular numbers.

What is the twentieth triangular number? $\left[\dfrac{(20)(21)}{2} = 210\right]$

n	1	2	3	4	. . .	n
number of dots	1	3	6	10	. . .	$\dfrac{(n) \times (n+1)}{2}$

Here is another way to explore the triangular number pattern. Write the following number pattern on the chalkboard:

```
1
2    3
4    5    6
7    8    9    10
11   12   13   14   15
...
...
46   47   48   49   50   51   52   53   54
```

Refer to the numbers in each row.

The last number in row 3 is 6.

What is the first number in row 8? [29]

How many numbers in row 15? [15]

What is the last number in row n? [$n(n + 1)/2$]

Pose other problems for the class to solve. Here is an example:

Suppose some towns wish to string fiber-optic cables so that each town is connected to every other town by exactly one cable. What is the relationship between the number of towns and the number of cables? Look for a pattern. Each of the 5 towns is connected to the other 4: $\dfrac{4 \times 5}{2} = 10$.

5 towns, 10 cables

$$\dfrac{4 \times 5}{2} = 10$$

Towns	2	3	4 . . . n
Cables	1	3	6 . . . $\dfrac{(n - 1) \times n}{2}$

The students should recognize the triangular numbers. Guide the students to see that the sequence starts with two towns.

FIBONACCI NUMBERS

Get ready. The purpose of this activity is to have students investigate Fibonacci numbers and explore some of the connections between these numbers and the golden ratio found in nature and architecture.

Students will need calculators, paper and pencil, and four cardboard rectangles (see *Keep going*). A ripe sunflower blossom and pine cones are helpful in illustrating how Fibonacci numbers occur in nature.

Get going. An Italian mathematician named Leonardo of Pisa (also called Fibonacci) discovered a sequence of numbers when he investigated the following problem:

How many pairs of rabbits can be produced each month in a year from a single pair if each adult pair gives birth to a new pair every month, each new pair reproduces from the second month on, and no rabbit dies?

Discuss this problem thoroughly so that everyone is clear on the facts as they are given and what question is to be answered. (How many pairs are produced each month in a year?) Have students solve the problem and be prepared to justify their solutions.

After the students have discussed their strategies, show them the following table if they have not already constructed it.

Month	Baby pairs produced each month	Adult pairs	Total pairs at end of month
1	1	1 (starting pair)	2
2	1	2	3
3	2	3	5
4	3	5	8
5	5	8	13
6	8	13	21
7	13	21	34
8	21	34	55
9	34	55	89
10	55	89	144
11	89	144	233
12	144	233	377

A = Adult pair   *Months*
b = baby pair

A	*Start*
b A	*Month 1*
A b A	*Month 2*
b A A b A	*Month 3*
A b A b A A b A	*Month 4*

The total number of pairs produced during the year is 376. (The original breeding pair is not counted.) Ask the students to identify any patterns they find.

This sequence of numbers, 1, 1, 2, 3, 5, 8, ..., continues in the pattern that Fibonacci described: the next number is the sum of the previous two numbers. Ask the students if they can continue the pattern to compute the number of pairs produced in two years. [161 392] Many examples of Fibonacci numbers are found in nature. The sunflower, for example, has two sets of spirals made up of the seeds on its blossom face. One set is clockwise, the other counterclockwise. The number of spirals are usually two consecutive Fibonacci numbers, for example, 13 and 21. Similarly, the spiral arms of scales on pine cones usually have five spiral arms in one direction and eight in the other. Some plants, for example the sneezewort, grow with a Fibonacci sequence of branches when viewed in a two-dimensional cross section: 1 main stem, 2 branches, 3 branches, 5 branches, 8 branches, and so on.

Keep going. Cut out four cardboard rectangles with the following dimensions:

A. 8 cm × 16 cm	C. 10 cm × 10 cm
B. 6 cm × 10 cm	D. 4 cm × 16 cm

Hold the four cards (labeled A, B, C, and D) for class inspection.

Which shape would you prefer for a note card? A picture frame? A picture window?

Allow the students time to consider each shape and to vote on their favorite. Ask for reasons why they chose a particular shape.

The ancient Greeks believed that the rectangular shape whose width-to-length ratio came closest to the "golden rectangle" was the most pleasing to the eye. The golden rectangle has the ratio of its width to its length equal to the ratio of its length to the sum of its width and length. This ratio (called the golden ratio) is an irrational number, 0.61803.... Both a 3-inch-by-5-inch index card and the front section of the Greek Parthenon have a width-to-length ratio that is close to the golden ratio.

Have the students use calculators to investigate the ratio of consecutive Fibonacci numbers.

Examples:

5	÷	8	=	(The display shows 0.625.)
8	÷	13	=	(The display shows 0.615.)
13	÷	21	=	(The display shows 0.619.)

Allow them time to investigate several ratios and then ask questions about the behavior of these ratios. One student may observe that the ratios are all close to 0.62. Another student may see that the ratios all begin with 0.6.

Do the ratios of consecutive Fibonacci numbers seem to get close to a certain number? [Yes; the number, to five decimal places, seems to be 0.61803.]

Consider a rectangle with dimensions 1 unit by 1.61803... units. Interestingly, if a square is removed from a golden rectangle, the remaining rectangle is also a golden rectangle.

The golden rectangle is used in packaging and advertising, as seen in these examples from the grocery shelves. Have your students look for other examples and discuss them in class. A survey of people's visual preference for one rectangle over another would make an interesting study for students. This data exploration could take many forms.

Because the square was assumed to have a length of 1 unit, the short side(s) of the new rectangle has a length of about $s = 1.61803 - 1$, or 0.61803 units. A square could be removed from this new rectangle, creating another golden rectangle, and so on, forever.

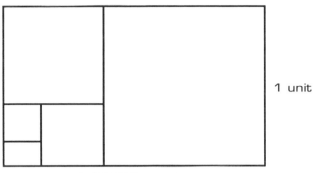

1.61803... units

Aesthetic appreciation for the golden ratio dates back not only to the ancient Greeks but also to the Egyptians. The Egyptian pyramids at Giza were built with an average base-to-height ratio of 8 to 5. The Greek Pythagoreans chose as their symbol the pentagram, a five-pointed star with a pentagon as its center. The pentagram is full of golden ratios.

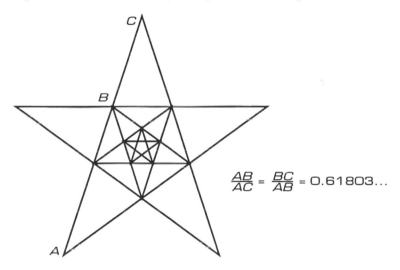

$$\frac{AB}{AC} = \frac{BC}{AB} = 0.61803\ldots$$

In a pentagram (five-pointed star), the ratio of the largest part of one side, *AB*, to the total side, *AC*, is equal to the ratio of *BC* to *AB*, and each ratio is equal to the golden ratio.

Seasoned teachers will attest to the fact that, given a mathematical question, some students give answers that are obviously far from correct, but they are not bothered at all by the discrepancy. The answer 114, for example, as a response to the product of 38 and 0.3 seems not to worry them at all. Such students either do not possess, or are not applying, number sense. It is not that they do not know their multiplication facts or cannot perform the algorithm; it is more likely that they have had little experience estimating answers, rarely think to check if the answers they obtain are reasonable, or do not understand place value.

Students with number sense pay attention to the meaning of numbers and operations and make realistic estimates of the results of computation. They can accurately select the appropriate unit to use when measuring and seem to be intuitively aware when an answer is "out of the ballpark." These abilities to deal sensibly with numbers are a strength both in and out of the classroom.

Number sense is a critical component of our students' education. Encouraging students to estimate and check answers as an integral part of any numerical exercise, discussing common measurement situations with them, and asking them to justify their mathematical choices will help these students develop this crucial ability. It would be best if such experiences were part of the curriculum from kindergarten on, but it is never too late to begin.

What could you measure with—

Millimeters?   Inches?   Miles?

piano keys   My Foot   DISTANCE TO GRANDMA'S
FILM   the desk   Distance to the moon
     My cat's tail

Feet?   Kilometers?

MY BED   Distance to Tommy's house
Width of classroom rug   How FAR THE SCHOOL BUS GOES

THE WORLD AROUND US

Get ready. The purpose of this activity is to have students practice estimating, ordering large numbers, and finding percentages with real-world data. The students' social studies teacher may wish to work with you in presenting this activity.

◆   ◆   ◆   ◆   ◆   ◆   ◆   ◆

Get going. Give pairs of students maps of the world, transparent centimeter grids, and a list of countries belonging to the United Nations. Together, select five countries to study. Have each pair locate the first designated country on the map. Using the map's scale and the centimeter grid, the students should estimate each country's area.

When the students have completed the task, find the class average and then consult a social studies textbook or other resource materials to see whether individual estimates or the average estimate is closer to the published figures. Repeat the activity to estimate the areas of the other four countries. Then ask the students to order the countries by area, using < and > signs. Encourage them to express the area in various ways, for example, 3 400 000 square kilometers or 3.4 million square kilometers.

Have the students select another country, find it on their maps, and, on the basis of their previous work, write down their estimates of its area.

Encourage class discussion by asking questions such as these:

Peter, how did you arrive at your estimate? Did anyone else use a different strategy? Show us how you did it.

Can you find a country about the same size as India? Portugal? Chile? Malaysia?

On the basis of what you have observed, how large do you think Europe is?

Keep going. Have the students use several years of population figures, obtained from such library reference materials as the *World Almanac*, to estimate a country's population for some year in the future, say, the year 2000. After this research has been completed, have each team use calculators to compute the estimated growth rate for each country.

Area models are especially helpful in visualizing numerical ideas from a geometric point of view. (NCTM 1989a, p. 88)

Some comments teachers might hear:
"Is England part of Europe?"
"Our grid isn't big enough."
"Let's use our calculators."
"The map scale is in inches but my grid is in centimeters."
"Let's divide it up."
"I'll take Germany."

The population density of the U.S. in 1980 was 64 people per square mile, and in 1990 it was 70 people per square mile.

As a writing assignment, ask the students to project and discuss what problems caused by the increased population density could arise by the year 2000.

◆　　◆　　◆　　◆　　◆　　◆　　◆　　◆

The data below may be used to help the class as a group practice finding projected growth rates.

Country	Population 1989	Projected population 2000
U.S.A.	248 800 000	268 100 000
China	1 103 900 000	1 255 700 000
France	56 100 000	57 100 000
Canada	26 300 000	29 400 000
South Africa	38 500 000	46 900 000

Source: *World Almanac 1990*

Assign the children to groups of four and give them the task of finding the population density of several countries of their choice by using the data they have obtained (the area of a country in square units and its population).

Give each pair of students a copy of a world map and ask them to choose a country, cut it out of the map, and mount it on construction paper to make a poster. Have them write beside the country its current population, the population growth rate, and the expected population in the year 2000. They may wish to look up the area of the country and compute the current population density and the projected population density. Depending on what is currently being discussed in social studies class, other data might also be entered on the poster.

GOING SHOPPING

Get ready. The purpose of this activity is to have students create and solve word problems by using real-world data.

Calculators should be available for student use. Bring in newspaper advertisements or furnish students with an enlarged copy of the chart below.

Summer Sporting Equipment	
Item	Cost
Skateboard	$ 96.59
Skateboard wheels	23.50 (set)
Skateboard knee pads	6.25 (pair)
Skateboard arm guards	8.95 (pair)
Surfboard	181.50
Boogie board	79.95
Goggles	17.50
Wet suit	124.99

Get going. Ask each student to write a story problem, using the data provided. Encourage them to be creative both in setting up the situation and in choosing the type of mathematical procedures required to solve the problem. When they have finished, have them exchange papers and attempt to solve the problem they receive.

As the students attempt to solve the problems, they may discover that further clarification and revisions are needed. Provide time for editing. Partners should communicate with each other, edit the problems as necessary, and solve them.

After an appropriate period, call on students to read the edited problems and discuss the process they used to find the solution. Having other class members suggest alternative strategies will enrich this activity for all your students. To strengthen problem-posing skills, repeat the activity.

Let the students write the problems using a computer and word processing software. If computers are not available, the students can create a story file by writing their problems on 4 x 6 index cards. Have them sort the problems into different categories: levels of difficulty, number of steps required to solve, and operations used. The sorting activity will give you insight into the kinds of problems the students are comfortable solving, the complexity of some students' work, and their sorting schemes. This information will help you better plan your mathematics lessons and learn more about each student in your class.

An interesting writing assignment for students' mathematics journals would be to have the students answer the following questions:

What kinds of problems are difficult to solve?

What makes a problem hard?

How can you tell when a problem is easy?

Keep going. You may wish to have students generate and share original problems based on similar data found in catalogs, menus, flyers, or newspaper ads. The problems can be shared by mail or by computer networking with other sixth graders. This activity will provide many opportunities for problem posing, editing, and solving.

BEAN CITY

Get ready. The purpose of this activity is to have students work with a situation that involves problem solving, estimating, and working with ratios.

> *By listening to students' ideas and encouraging them to listen to one another, one can establish an atmosphere of mutual respect. (NCTM 1989a, p. 69)*

> *Data bases and computer programs can engage students in posing and solving problems. (NCTM 1989a, p. 76)*

> *Assessments should determine students' ability to perform all aspects of problem solving. Evidence about their ability to ask questions, use given information, and make conjectures is essential to determine if they can formulate problems. (NCTM 1989a, p. 209)*

This Bean City activity creates a need for students to use ratios and is a logical introduction to the topic.

Bean City Samples

Sample	Navy	Pinto	Lima
A	3	5	2
B	4	8	3
C	2	6	1

Estimate of navy beans:

$9/34 = ?/1000$

$? = 9000/34$ navy beans

Overheard in the class:

Tomeka said, "Just take half for 50 percent."

Mary said, "I take 10 percent of 17 instead of 17 percent of 10."

Marea said, "If it is over 100 percent, I know the answer is greater than what I started with."

Jose said, "I use fractional equivalents whenever I can. If I want 25 percent of 16, I take 1/4 of 16."

Have available an assortment of weighing and measuring devices, then distribute to each group of four to six students an opaque bag filled with 1000 beans of mixed variety. Navy beans, pinto beans, and lima beans work well. Each group also needs one copy of the Bean City Census planning sheet (p. 15).

Get going. Tell the students that they are to act as census takers to determine the proportion of each kind of bean in Bean City, a small town with a population of 1000. However, they must sample the population, since the city council of Bean City is not willing to pay for a door-to-door census (an exact count). Guide the students in planning a sampling strategy.

You may wish to have a student list all the sampling suggestions on an overhead transparency or on the chalkboard. Discuss some of the suggested sampling procedures with the students and encourage them to carry out a variety of them using their beans. If the students do not suggest weighing as a possibility, prompt them to include this as a strategy.

As the students decide on a strategy and begin working on the Bean City census, suggest that they assign the job of scribe to one of their members. It will be the scribe's responsibility to document the results of the group's discussions, record the way they carry out their sampling procedure, and fill in the planning sheet.

Keep going. As groups complete their census, have them briefly discuss their estimates. Allow them to count the beans and to compare their estimates with the count. Briefly report the results from each group and have the students comment on which sampling strategies seemed to give the most accurate picture of the bean population. You will want to encourage the students to reflect on what happened in each group.

A bulletin board devoted to this activity will encourage the students to depict their data in several ways. Some students could write "newspaper" articles for the bulletin board; others could write editorials about the efficiency of different sampling techniques or write advertisements for different survey companies.

FIND IT FAST

Get ready. The purpose of this activity is to have students sharpen their ability to find percentages mentally.

Get going. Write on an overhead transparency or on the chalkboard the following percentage expressions, one at a time:

50 percent of 30;	10 percent of 12
20 percent of 50;	150 percent of 40
17 percent of 10;	13 percent of 10
40 percent of 75;	35 percent of 20
16 percent of 25;	62 percent of 50
125 percent of 40;	30 percent of 50

Ask the students to generate a quick way to compute the answer and to explain why the shortcut works.

Keep going. Encourage the students to generate percentage exercises that can be solved mentally and to share them with their classmates at the beginning or the end of class.

BEAN CITY CENSUS

Census takers: _____ _____ _____ _____

There are 1000 beans in Bean City. Each bean belongs to one of these families: Navy, Pinto, or Lima. As a census taker, you need to plan how you will find out how many beans belong to each family. Describe your plan and carry it out.

Our Plan

Carry out your plan. Use the work space.

Work Space

Predictions

Number of Beans:

Pinto _____

Lima _____

Navy _____

MAKING SENSE OF DATA

...Instruction in statistics should focus on the active involvement of students in the entire process: formulating key questions; collecting and organizing data; representing the data using graphs, tables, frequency distributions, and summary statistics; analyzing the data; making conjectures; and communicating information in a convincing way.
(NCTM 1989a, p. 105)

There are many opportunities to include statistics in the sixth-grade curriculum. In so doing, students review many mathematical ideas, relate mathematics to the real world, and extend their ideas about statistics.

As students progress through the entire process—from formulating questions to communicating the results—they need some specific skills. The Going in Circles activity shows one way to build the skill of making a circle graph. Just as important, it illustrates how you can make connections to such other mathematical ideas as fractions, percents, and angle measure and to other subject areas such as social studies.

Often, students are asked to determine the mean (the arithmetic average), the median (the middle number), and the mode (the most frequent number), but they do not know why they are finding these summary statistics. The suggested activities provide students the opportunity to explore the relationship between the measures of central tendency. This is not an introduction to these ideas but a more in-depth study that will be enhanced by such questions as "What if?" "Can that happen?" "When would a mode be a good description of a set of data?" "Why do you suppose the mean is used?"

Other ideas that you may wish students to explore are how faulty arguments or misleading graphs can be based on data, how the use of spreadsheets can help analyze data, how computer programs can present data, and how data is sometimes misrepresented. The fact that there are no probability activities in this section should not imply that they are not important at this level. On the contrary, they furnish excellent examples of the use of fractions and percents, they involve students, and they are a source of data to be analyzed. You are encouraged to use other activities with probability experiments.

Going into a circle graph

GOING IN CIRCLES

Get ready. The purpose of this activity is to have children explore circle graphs as a way to represent data. The circle graph is used to represent data when the whole is known or can be predicted from a sample and questions are to be answered about the relative sizes of the parts of the whole.

The activity could be extended for many days. Remember that you are teaching more than how to make a circle graph. Students could also learn about percentages and angle measure. The theme for this activity is social studies, beginning with the population of the class and extending to the population of the world.

Materials needed are centimeter rulers and long paper strips about 2 centimeters wide and 100 centimeters long. Strips can be made from adding-machine tape folded lengthwise into halves or thirds. Have the students make a meter strip by marking one of the paper strips into centimeters from 1 to 100. Make several meter strips for yourself.

Each group will need paper and pencils or markers. If you connect this activity to angle measure, they will need protractors.

Get going. Brainstorm with the class about questions to ask their classmates; make a list of their ideas. Choose one idea for the class to pursue together and record their opinions.

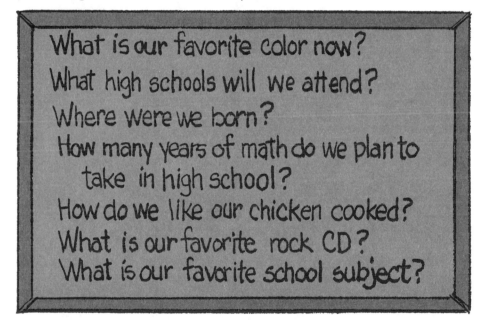

What is our favorite color now?
What high schools will we attend?
Where were we born?
How many years of math do we plan to take in high school?
How do we like our chicken cooked?
What is our favorite rock CD?
What is our favorite school subject?

Suppose the class chooses the following question to investigate: "How many years of mathematics do you plan to take in high school?" After a discussion that should conclude with the observations that everyone must take at least two years and that it is possible to take five years, have the students write on a piece of paper the number of years of mathematics that they think they will take. Suppose the opinion poll revealed the following student plans:

2 years	8 students
3 years	11 students
4 years	4 students
5 years	3 students

> *Data can be presented in many forms: charts, tables, plots (e.g., stem-and-leaf, box-and-whiskers, and scatter), and graphs (e.g., bar, circle, or line). Each form has a different impact on the picture of the information being presented, and each conveys a different perspective. The choice of form depends on the questions that are to be answered. (NCTM 1989a, p. 106)*

The students could first make a human graph by standing in a circle with the teacher in the center holding the strings that showed the divisions on the circle graph.

Next, let the students use their meter strips to show the data. The students will need to decide how many centimeters should be used to represent each student. For example, if there are twenty-six students in the class, every three centimeters on the 100-centimeter strip could represent a student. Mark the strip as shown, then show how the strip can be curved into a circle and the divisions marked to form a pie chart:

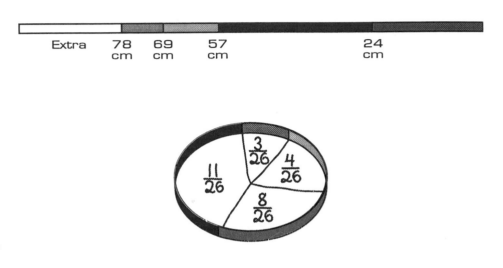

One teacher commented that the students' graphs were rather rough, but that the activity gave them insight into how to make circle graphs. She extended the lesson to connect fractions with percents and angle measures so that the students could make circle graphs without the strips.

Notice that eight students represent 24 percent of the whole meter strip, not 24 percent of the class. These eight students represent 8/26, or about 31 percent, of the class.

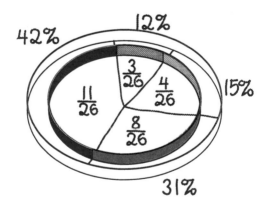

Percentages of 1990 seniors who took two to five years of mathematics:

2 years	34 percent
3 years	49 percent
4 years	14 percent
5 years	3 percent

When you have talked about this graph and labeled it, let each group choose a question, survey the class, and make a graph with paper strips. Have them transfer the graphs to construction paper. The groups should discuss what they have found.

Discuss when a circle graph is appropriate, such as when presenting the parts of a whole so they can be easily compared or when presenting a limited number of parts so each can be seen. Question why a circle graph would be inappropriate for representing such things as trends over time or different people's scores on a test.

Keep going. Have the students compare their plans for how many years of mathematics they will take to the amount of mathematics taken in the United States as a whole.

Since your students' data are expressed in terms of fractions and the nation's data in percentages, it will be helpful to express both as percentages. Return to the strip graph that you made and put a 100-centimeter strip around the outside as shown. This strip forms a concentric circle around the first one. Extend the pie wedges until they meet the 100-centimeter tape. Now you can read the percentages off the 100-centimeter strip and compare the class's results to the nation's. How do they compare?

Have the groups find the percentages for the graphs they made and, if possible, compare their results with those of another class. If the other class has a different number of students, the fractional parts may be difficult to compare, but the percentages will be easy!

Another avenue to take is to relate circle graphs to the degrees in a circle. Pose the problem of how to represent on a circle graph the population of the world by continents. Display the following information:

North America	8	percent
South America	6	percent
Europe	14	percent
Asia	60	percent
Africa	12	percent

(All other areas are less than 1 percent.)

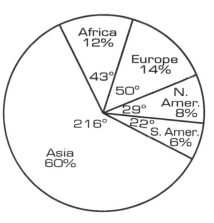

World Population

Discuss with the students how they could make the graph. One way is to use the 100-centimeter strip, another is to use a computer program, and a third is to use angle measures. Have the students sketch what they think the graph will look like. Certainly, Asia should cover more than half of the circle and Europe and Africa will be about the same size, as will North and South America. Show the students how to make in the circle a central angle of 29 degrees (8 percent of 360 degrees) for North America, and so forth, as illustrated.

Other information is available in almanacs. Some examples that may be selected and graphed follow:

percentage of the earth that each continent occupies
percentage of the population in each age bracket in the United States
percentage of each ethnic group in Canada (or in other countries)

GETTING TO THE CENTER OF THINGS

Get ready. The purpose of this activity is to have the children find the mean, the mode, and the median from data given in a graph. The activity assumes that your students are familiar with these descriptions of data. If not, you will need to do some background work with them before using these ideas.

Each student will need a copy of High Jump Trials (p. 23) and a calculator.

Get going. Begin a group discussion of the graphs on the High Jump Trials worksheet with such questions as the following:

What information does each graph give us?

Did all the girls make the same number of jumps?

Who jumped the highest most often?

Can you tell the mode by just looking at the graph? How about the median? How about the mean?

(It should be easy to find the mode on each graph; several have more than one mode. The median is also not difficult to estimate from the graphs, since the scores are in order. The mean is more difficult to determine, since a square at 58 represents a different height than a square at 62.)

Can you look at the graph and tell whether the mean will be more or less than 60?

Although this activity is based on data given to the students, it should be enriched by having the students think about and discuss what they are doing. Without such discussion, the activity misses the spirit of the Curriculum and Evaluation Standards entirely.

One class heatedly discussed who they thought would win the actual contest. About half the students chose Misoslava because she jumped more 61- and 62-inch jumps in the trials and also had the highest mean. Others thought Mildred would win because when she was "on," she could jump 62 inches consistently. There was no way for the students to settle the discussion, so they decided to collect some real data from the high school track team.

Let the students complete the table and the questions on the worksheet. Students may not be familiar with taking the data from the graph to find the mean (the average). Some may fail to realize, for example, that Misoslava had two jumps of 59 inches and three jumps of 60 inches. One way to find her average is shown on the High Jump Trials worksheet.

After the students have completed their work, discuss what they have found and return to the beginning set of questions to see if they look at these any differently.

Keep going. Extend the activity by posing other questions:

Do symmetric graphs always have the same mean as median?

What happens to the mean if there is one very high jump, but all the other jumps are like Sara's? What happens to the median then?

Students are often interested in how final grades are determined. Have the students decide whether they would like their mean or their median grade to be the final grade for a marking period.

What if you had five grades of 82 and one of 34?

What if you had grades of 80, 80, 82, 99, and 100? How about 80, 80, 97, 98, 100? Is the mean or the median a better description of your total work?

Why isn't the mode used? Should it be used?

Have the students make up a problem in which the mode may be an appropriate measure to use and let them defend their choice.

WHAT DATA?

Get ready. Often students are given data or collect data and then find the mean (arithmetic average), the median (middle number), and the mode (most frequent number). In this activity, they are given these and the lowest and highest numbers; they are to find the data from which these numbers could have come. No special equipment is needed for this activity, although you may want to have connecting cubes available to reinforce an understanding of the mean.

Pieces of candy for 9 people	
Lowest number	**0**
Highest number	**9**
Mean	**4**
Median	**4**
Mode	**2**

Get going. Present the following situation to the students:

Nine people have some candy. The most anyone has is 9 pieces. At least one person has no candy. The average (mean) number of pieces is 4. Four is also the median. That means at least one person has 4 pieces. More people have 2 pieces of candy than any other number.

If students need help after trying to solve the problem, provide connecting cubes or other objects for them to use. Encourage the students to talk through the problem by asking questions that will elicit responses such as those illustrated below:

Miranda said, "A mean of 4 means that each person would receive 4 candies if everyone had the same amount. There are 9 people."

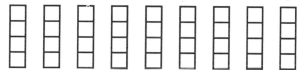

Joel explained, "The low is 0 and the high is 9, so I'll take 5 cubes and make the high 9. I took one of these from another low stack."

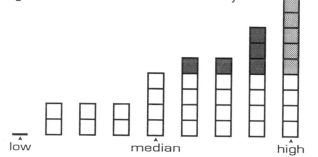

Lavinia declared, "The mode is 2 so I must have more stacks with 2. I'll try making all the low stacks have 2. That will give me 5 cubes to put on the high side. Gee, it worked the first try."

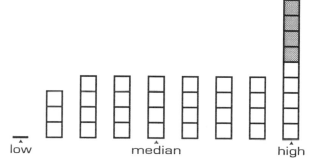

John interrupted, "But I see there are other ways. I could have two stacks of 4 and a 6 instead of the 5."

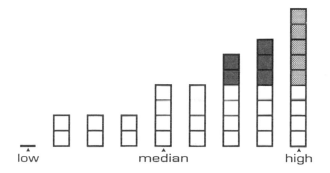

Now present the following information to the students:

> Nine apple baskets are in the cafeteria. No basket has more than 9 apples; in fact, some baskets may be empty. The mean number of apples in the baskets is 4, the median is 4, and the mode is 2. How many apples are needed to solve the problem, and how could they be distributed among the baskets? Find a set of data that could be described by this information.

Some possible solutions:

0, 1, 2, 2, 4, 5, 6, 7, 9

0, 2, 2, 2, 4, 4, 6, 7, 9

0, 2, 2, 2, 4, 5, 5, 7, 9

0, 2, 2, 2, 4, 5, 6, 6, 9

2, 2, 2, 2, 4, 4, 6, 6, 8

Have the children tell how they would distribute the apples.

In this example, there are several correct solutions, some of which are shown at the left.

Ask the students why the following answers would be incorrect:

> 0, 0, 2, 2, 4, 5, 6, 8, 9
> [0 is also a mode.]
>
> 0, 1, 2, 3, 4, 5, 6, 6, 9
> [2 is not a mode.]
>
> 0, 2, 2, 2, 5, 5, 6, 7, 7
> [4 is not the median.]
>
> 0, 1, 2, 2, 4, 5, 6, 8, 9
> [4 is not the mean.]
>
> 2, 2, 2, 2, 4, 4, 4, 6, 10
> [10 is too many.]

	Billy	Rose	Lou
Number of data points	7	9	9
Lowest number	0	1	9
Highest number	9	9	9
Mean	4	5⅓	8
Median	4	5	6
Mode	6	8	7
Number of solutions	one	many	none

Keep going. Have the students make up their own mystery set of data and find the mode, the mean, the median, and the highest and the lowest numbers. Then have them display these as shown at the left as a challenge for other students. See if some students can make up a data set with only one solution (see Billy's) or with no possible solution (see Lou's).

Have the students investigate what happens if one of the central measures (mean, mode, or median) is not given. Are more or fewer solutions possible?

Ask the students to choose seven to ten scores for a set of hypothetical quizzes they have taken and to answer the following question:

> If the teacher uses different measures of central tendency to determine the final grade, show that the set of quiz grades produces different final grades for the student. Explain your rationale.

HIGH JUMP TRIALS

During a practice for the Olympic high jump, each athlete had 15 trial jumps. The following graphs show the number of times each athlete jumped a distance from 58 to 62 inches. For example, lolanda jumped 60 inches on 5 trials.

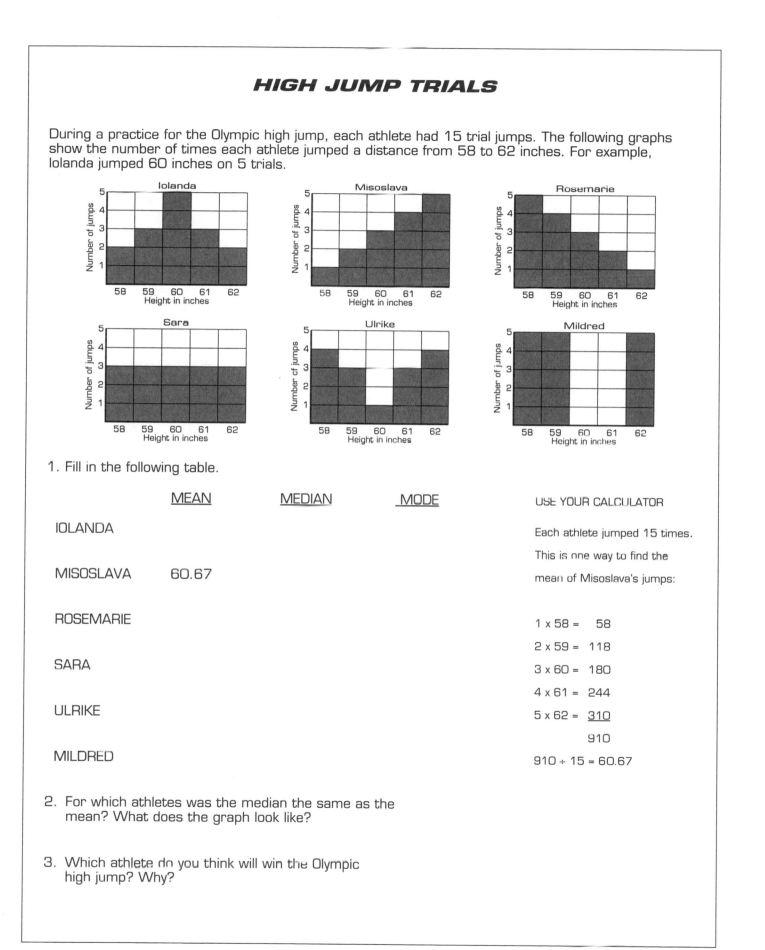

1. Fill in the following table.

	MEAN	MEDIAN	MODE
IOLANDA			
MISOSLAVA	60.67		
ROSEMARIE			
SARA			
ULRIKE			
MILDRED			

USE YOUR CALCULATOR

Each athlete jumped 15 times. This is one way to find the mean of Misoslava's jumps:

1 x 58 =   58
2 x 59 = 118
3 x 60 = 180
4 x 61 = 244
5 x 62 = <u>310</u>
        910

910 ÷ 15 = 60.67

2. For which athletes was the median the same as the mean? What does the graph look like?

3. Which athlete do you think will win the Olympic high jump? Why?

GEOMETRY AND SPATIAL SENSE

The study of geometry in grades 5–8 links the inform-al explorations begun in grades K–4 to the more formalized processes studied in grades 9–12. (NCTM 1989a, p. 112)

This does not imply that the study of geometry in grades 5–8 should be a formalized endeavor; rather, it should simply provide increased opportunities for students to engage in more syste-matic explorations. (NCTM 1989a, p. 112)

Although many sixth-grade students are capable of dealing with abstractions, the focus of these activities is still strongly on concrete and pictorial experiences. It is through the use of models that children develop the concepts necessary to make abstractions and generalizations. Hands-on and activity-based experiences are remembered and are precisely those that are required to enable students to improve their level of geometric sophistication. In grade 6, students are given an opportunity to increase the number of concepts in their repertoire and to illustrate how these concepts can be used in geometric reasoning.

Although many activities are suitable for whole-class participation, a lack of sufficient materials may make this difficult. Therefore, several activities are written for a mathematics center or for small-group work. Whether you plan whole-class instruction or activity centers, students should have many opportunities to work together, share ideas, talk about mathematics, stimulate and encourage each other, and draw shared conclusions through analysis and discussion. The model of cooperative learning that is used is optional.

Since geometry is the study of objects, motions, and relationships in a spatial environment, it is only natural to relate the drawing of plane figures to the motions of oneself or to the motions of an object such as a turtle. This helps children connect the physical to the abstract world. For example, determining what path a turtle will draw when given a sequence of Logo commands helps students internalize their own physical actions.

SORTING QUADRILATERALS

Get ready. The purpose of this activity is to have students explore some of the basic properties of a variety of quadrilaterals. Drawing and identifying quadrilaterals involve the spatial abilities of visualization and of mentally flipping and turning figures to test for congruency.

Give the students geopaper (p. 32) divided into 3 x 3 sections. Explain that only one quadrilateral should be drawn on each array of nine dots. The students may wish to use tracing paper to test figures for congruency.

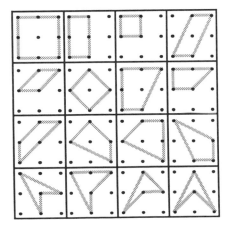

Get going. Have the students find and draw on the geopaper as many noncongruent quadrilaterals as they can. They should use a different set of dots for each figure. (The sixteen possible figures are shown at the left.)

The students may have greater success finding all sixteen figures if they work in groups. Encourage the students to identify duplicates by tracing one figure and matching the tracing to the duplicate. Have the students identify different noncongruent figures.

How many different squares are there?

Show me a trapezoid. Is there another one?

How many different concave quadrilaterals can you find?

Have the students make a set of drawings of all sixteen quadrilaterals

Using color to indicate parallel or congruent segments avoids introducing more symbols and gives a strong visual reinforcement.

and sort the figures into groups. Have the class discuss and explain the different sorting categories they used.

Keep going. Have the students sort the quadrilaterals into sets of convex and concave figures. They should draw the diagonals of each figure and note that for each concave figure, one diagonal is outside the figure. Have them test this property of concave figures by drawing other concave polygons and their diagonals.

Wrap a string around a polygon. What difference do you see between concave and convex polygons?

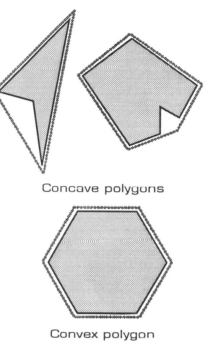

Concave polygons

Convex polygon

DIAGONAL PROPERTIES OF QUADRILATERALS

Get ready. The purposes of this activity are to have students extend their knowledge of the properties of quadrilaterals and to explore the properties related to the diagonals of quadrilaterals.

In previous grades, many students have had experience in intuitively establishing geometric properties of figures and geometric facts by using manipulatives. Slides, flips, and turns of objects and the properties of the motions themselves help form the beginning of a sound foundation for the study of geometry in later grades.

In this activity, the properties of figures under a reflection or a turn are explored. In particular, the line and turn symmetries of quadrilaterals are investigated.

A figure has turn symmetry if the figure and its turn image coincide after a specified turn. This also shows that a figure and its turn image are congruent.

To describe a turn completely, you need a turn center and the angle of rotation or turn. In this activity, turns are restricted to one-quarter (90°), one-half (180°), and three-quarters (270°). All turns in this activity are clockwise turns.

Students may recognize that a four-sided figure with three right angles must have four right angles. Encourage students to make larger drawings of the quadrilaterals and to measure the angles of each figure. "What do you notice about the sums of the angles?"

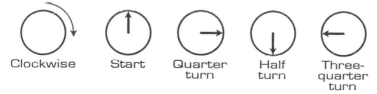

Clockwise Start Quarter turn Half turn Three-quarter turn

The lines of symmetry of a square meet at the center of the square.

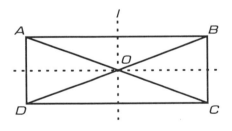

Materials required for this activity are dot or grid paper and tracing paper, tissue paper, or acetate.

Get going. Have each student draw a large square on dot paper or grid paper. Ask them to draw the four lines of symmetry of the square and use paper folding or a mirror to check.

Where do the lines of symmetry intersect?

Have them trace a copy of their square and its lines of symmetry onto tissue or tracing paper or a piece of acetate. Mark the center, *O*, of the square.

Place the copy on top of the original square. Rotate the copy about the center *O* by lightly pressing a pencil or any sharp pointed object on the copy at *O*, holding the original drawing in place, and turning the copy.

Have the students verify that the copy and the original square coincide (fit exactly over one another) after a quarter, half, or three-quarter turn.

The square has quarter-turn, half-turn, and three-quarter turn symmetry.

Ask the students to repeat the activity with an equilateral triangle, a rectangle, a regular pentagon, and a regular hexagon, finding their turn symmetries.

Have the students draw a rectangle of their choice with its diagonals and two lines of symmetry. Have them trace a copy of their rectangle onto tissue paper or a piece of acetate.

Does a rectangle have quarter-turn symmetry? Half-turn symmetry? [No; Yes]

Fold the rectangle along the line l.

How does this show that AO = OB? DO = OC?

How does this show that AC = BD?

Have the students use a half-turn about *O* to answer the following questions:

How does this show that AO = OC? BO = OD?

What can you say about AC and BD on the basis of this half-turn? [They bisect each other.]

Are the diagonals perpendicular? How can you show this? [Fold along *BD*. *AO* and *OC* do not coincide. Students may choose to measure the angles.]

As a further extension, investigate with your students the rhombus, the parallelogram, the kite, and the arrowhead. [Answers will be found in the chart on page 27.]

Keep going. The following chart summarizes the properties of quadrilaterals. Make a similar chart (without the entries) on the chalkboard and assign groups of students to complete the chart. One group is assigned the properties of a square, a second the properties of a rectangle, and so on. When the chart is completed, discuss it with the whole class.

	square	rectangle	parallelogram	rhombus	trapezoid	kite	arrowhead
No. of pairs of congruent sides	2	2	2	2	0*	2	2
No. of pairs of parallel sides	2	2	2	2	1	0	0
Diagonals are congruent.	yes	yes	no	no	no*	no	no
Diagonals bisect each other.	yes	yes	yes	yes	no	no**	no**
Diagonals are perpendicular.	yes	no	no	yes	no	yes	yes
Has half-turn symmetry.	yes	yes	yes	yes	no	no	no
Number of lines of symmetry	4	2	0	2	0*	1	1
Other properties	For example, pairs of congruent angles, right angles, and so on.						

* An isosceles trapezoid has the following properties: its diagonals are equal in length and it has one line of symmetry. However, these properties cannot be generalized to any trapezoid.

**One diagonal bisects the other, but not the reverse.

To encourage deductive reasoning and generalizations, ask questions such as these:

Are all squares rectangles? Are all rectangles squares?

Are all rectangles parallelograms? Are all parallelograms rectangles?

Have the students justify and defend their answers.

LOGO AND THE PROPERTIES OF REGULAR FIGURES

Get ready. The purposes of this activity are to have children—

- find the sum of the measures of the exterior angles of any polygon;
- find the angle measure of each exterior angle in a regular polygon;
- write algorithms or procedures that draw regular polygons.

Students should know how to use a protractor and be familiar with a 360° angle. If a computer is not available, have the students "act out" the motions of the Logo turtle.

Make sure the students realize that the number of interior angles of a plane figure equals the number of vertices of the figure; that there are two sets of exterior angles; and that in each set, the number of exterior angles equals the number of vertices of the figure.

Writing Logo programs can be quite tedious when instructions have to be repeated many times. A convenient shortcut is available in the Logo

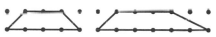

Isoceles trapezoid　　　Trapezoid

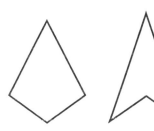

Kite　　　Arrowhead

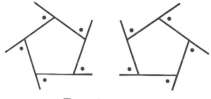

• Exterior angles

language. For example, to draw a square with sides 80 steps long we can write

> REPEAT 4 [FD 80 RT 90].

This instructs the computer to repeat the commands FD 80 and RT 90 *four* times.

TO SQUARE
FD 80
RT 90
FD 80
RT 90
FD 80
RT 90
FD 80
RT 90

The heading TO SQUARE names the program and, if used as a command, will make the turtle draw a square with sides 80 steps long once the program has been entered.

Materials required for this activity are rulers, protractors, and a computer with the Logo computer language.

Get going. Ask the students to visualize themselves walking around a four-sided polygon. Ask them through what total angle their body turns in walking around the figure and returning to the starting point. [360°] Check the answer by the having the students walk around a four-sided figure drawn on the floor. They should end by facing as at the beginning and should have turned completely around once.

Would the sum of the turns be any different if the polygon were five-sided? Six-sided? One hundred-sided? [No]

Check by having a student walk around a five-sided figure and a six-sided figure.

Would changing the lengths of the sides of the polygon change the sum of the turn angles? Explain. [No, the lengths of the sides affect the number of steps taken but not the amount of turn at each vertex.]

Demonstrate the following procedure on an overhead projector or have the students draw a quadrilateral of their choice and follow the instructions given.

> Lay a pencil on your paper and place it with the eraser end on a vertex of the quadrilateral, pointing along one side. Slide the pencil along that side until the eraser is on the next vertex, and turn the pencil so that it is pointing along the next side. Continue sliding to the next corner and turning until the pencil reaches the starting position.

Through what angle does the pencil turn in its journey from start to finish? [360°]

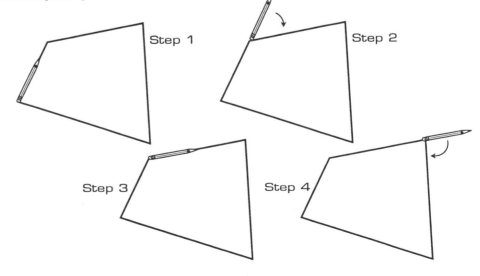

Step 1　Step 2

Step 3　Step 4

Every classroom will have at least one computer available at all times for demonstrations and student use. Additional computers should be available for individual, small-group, and whole class use. (NCTM 1989a, p. 68)

The angles through which the pencil turns are the exterior angles of the quadrilateral.

Make a true statement about the sum of the exterior angles of a quadrilateral.

Relate turning the pencil to turning your body as you walk around a polygon.

The set of diagrams below illustrates that the sum of the exterior angles of a quadrilateral is 360°. Have the students explain why this is so.

[Visualize the quadrilateral collapsing to a point as the sides slide toward that point. The exterior angles remain unchanged. The final diagram shows that the sum of the exterior angles is 360°.]

The same technique used with a pentagon or a hexagon shows that the sum of the exterior angles will always be 360°.

THE INCREDIBLE SHRINKING QUADRILATERAL

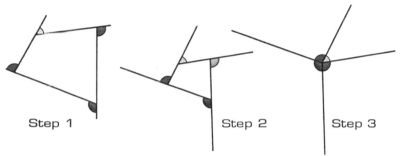

Step 1   Step 2   Step 3

The side lengths remain unchanged as they slide toward the center point. If color is available, the sides can be distinguished using color.

Ask each student to copy the program at the right, which is a procedure to draw an equilateral triangle. Ask the students to estimate or calculate the amount of turn at each vertex and to test their guess by running the program. If they do not get an equilateral triangle, they should try again.

```
TO EQTRI
FD  50
RT  ——  [120]
FD  50
RT  ——  [120]
FD  50
RT  ——  [120]
```

What is the angle through which the turtle turns at each vertex as it traces out (a) a square [360 ÷ 4], (b) a regular pentagon [360 ÷ 5], (c) a regular hexagon [360 ÷ 6]?

Write a Logo procedure to draw each of the following regular polygons with sides of length 50 steps: (a) a square, (b) a pentagon, (c) a hexagon, (d) an octagon.

Keep going. Have the children write a procedure to draw the pattern illustrated below.

First, write a procedure, TO OCT: start at A, trace all the way around a regular octagon whose sides are 30 steps long, and continue to B again. Then, use TO OCT to draw the whole pattern. Note that you need commands to get from x to y.

Discuss the importance of the figure being a regular polygon.

Answer:

(a) REPEAT 4 [FD 50 RT 90]

(b) REPEAT 5 [FD 50 RT 72]

(c) REPEAT 6 [FD 50 RT 60]

(d) REPEAT 8 [FD 50 RT 45]

Answer:
```
TO OCT
REPEAT 13 [FD 30  RT 45]
END
TO PATTERN
REPEAT 3 [OCT  RT 135]
LT 135
FD 30
LT 90
FD 30
RT 45
REPEAT 3 [OCT  RT 135]
END
PATTERN
```

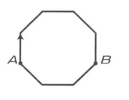

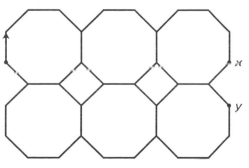

Linking cubes can be used to build the playing pieces.

SPACE PERCEPTION–PROBLEM SOLVING

Get ready. The purpose of this activity is to have children develop strategies involving the mental manipulation of figures.

Spatial thinking is an important part of an elementary school program. There is a connection between spatial thinking and mathematics, and studies in geometry vividly show that students weak in manipulating figures mentally find it difficult to follow the simplest arguments. A game situation is ideally suited to encourage students to develop strategies.

Have the students make game boards and game pieces out of tagboard. Patterns for the game board and pieces are on page 31.

Cut out six of each of the game pieces (1 to 6). It is helpful but not necessary to color code the pieces. For example, 1 could be white; 2, orange; 3, green; 4, red; 5, yellow; and 6, blue.

Get going. Explain the game to the students:

- Each player has a game board.
- Player A rolls two dice or number cubes marked 1 through 6. Suppose she rolls a 2 and a 6.
- Player A chooses either a 6-piece or a 2-piece and places it on her board. A piece may not be moved once it is placed.
- Player B rolls the two cubes. For example, he rolls a 3 and a 3.
- Player B has no choice but to use a 3-piece on his board. However, player B gets another turn because he rolled a double.
- As long as players roll doubles, their turn continues.
- As the board fills, the number of possible plays diminishes. For example, suppose player A has room for a 1-, a 2-, or a 3-piece only and rolls a 4 and a 5. Player A has two choices: to lose a turn or to use that turn to remove one of the pieces already on the board. No piece is added during the same turn.
- The first player to fill his or her board completely wins the game.

Keep going. Have the children play variations of the game:

Use alternative game pieces. For example, replace the 3-, 4-, 5-, and 6-pieces with figures 3A, 4A, 5A, and 6A.

Use an 8 x 8 game board.

Add the rule that to win, a player must have at least one piece of every color on the board. If the game pieces are not colored, the rule could demand one piece of each size.

Add the rule that no two pieces of the same color may touch except at a corner.

Store the game board and pieces in an envelope, suitably labeled, for future use.

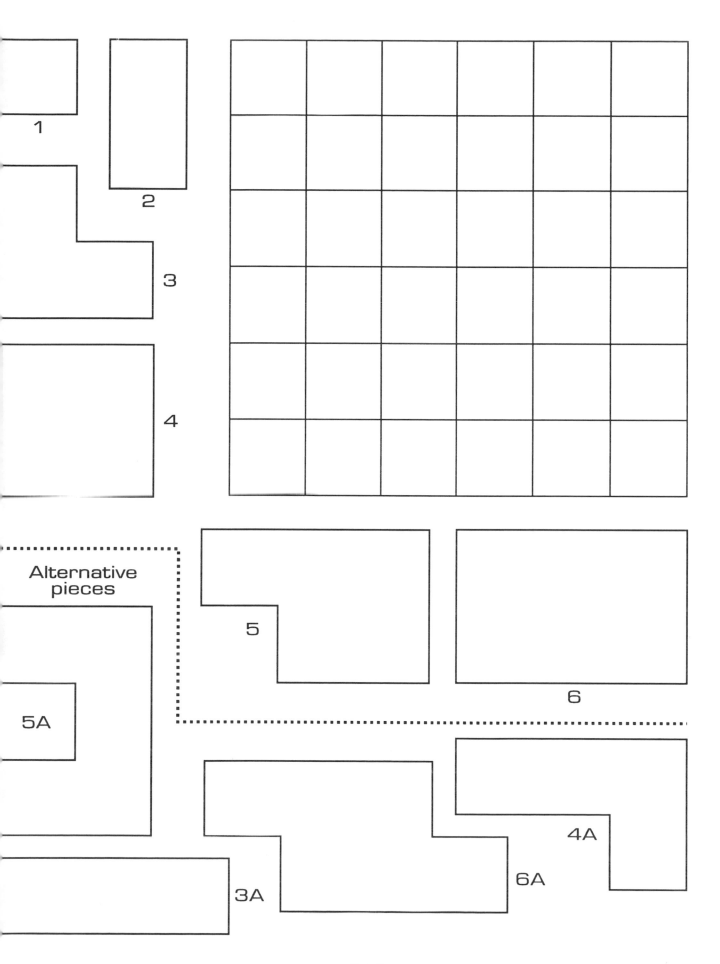

1

2

3

4

Alternative pieces

5A

5

6

3A

6A

4A